Driven from the Land

The Story of the Dust Bowl

GREAT JOURNEYS

Driven from the Land

The Story of the Dust Bowl

by Milton Meltzer

BENCHMARK BOOKS

MARSHALL CAVENDISH
NEW YORK

With special thanks to Robert D. Johnston,
Department of History, Yale University,
for his careful reading of this manuscript.

Benchmark Books
Marshall Cavendish Corporation
99 White Plains Road
Tarrytown, NY 10591-9001

Cover photograph: *A family's truck is stalled on the road between Dallas and Austin, Texas,
in August 1936.*

Photo research by Candlepants Incorporated
Cover photo: Corbis-Bettmann
The photographs in this book are used by permission and through the courtesy of:
UPI/CORBIS-Bettmann: 2–3, 18 (bottom), 27, 32, 38, 39, 40, 45, 49, 52, 74 (top), 77,
85, 87 (top & bottom), 89, 90, 92. *Library of Congress*: USF34-4047E, 8; USF34-16861-
C, 14; USF33-11274 M2, 25 (left); USF 3301-00428-M2, 25 (right); F342701-10124,
34; USF34-17956-C, 36; USF34-18283-C, 47; USZ62-11491, 50; USF34-16910-E, 54;
USF34-2701-16453, 57; USF34-9058-C,60; USZ62-19804, 66; USZ62-29223, 68;
USZ62-29223, 68; USZ62-46280, 70; USF33-2021-M1, 71; USF34-18607, 76;
USF34-16113, 79; USF34TOS 16336, 101. *The Dorothea Lange Collection, The Oakland
Museum of California, The City of Oakland. Gift of Paul S. Taylor*: 38258, 10; 66.179.24, 15;
33001, 20; 34013, 30; 38196, 56; 34102, 59; 38266, 82; 42084.4, 98;
CORBIS-Bettmann: 17, 18(top), 23, 28, 42, 74(bottom), 86. *National Archives*:
83-G-24-41542, 64. *UWE Walz/CORBIS*: 97.

Library of Congress Cataloging-in-Publication Data
Meltzer, Milton, 1915–
Driven from the land : the story of the Dust Bowl / by Milton Meltzer.
p.   cm. — (Great journeys)
Includes bibliographical references and index.
Summary: Describes the economic and environmental conditions that led to the
Great Depression and the horrific dust storms that drove people from their homes
westward during the 1930s.
ISBN 0-7614-0968-8 (lib. bdg.)
1. Dust storms—Great Plains—History—20th century—Juvenile literature.
2. Droughts—Great Plains—History—20th century—Juvenile literature.
3. Great Plains—Social conditions—Juvenile literature. 4. Great Plains—
Economic conditions—Juvenile literature. 5. Migration, Internal—United States—
History—20th century—Juvenile literature. 6. West (U.S.)—History—1890–1945—
Juvenile literature. 7. Depressions—1929—Great Plains—Juvenile literature.
[1. Dust storms—Great Plains.   2. Droughts—Great Plains—History.
3. Depressions—1929.]   I. Series.
F595.M55   2000   978—dc21   98-47501   CIP   AC

Printed in the United States of America

1 3 5 6 4 2

Contents

Also by Milton Meltzer

Foreword

THE WIND RISES, AND SUDDENLY ALL MOVEMENT STOPS. THE SURFACE OF the land floats up, and thick clouds of dust darken the sun. Drivers in their automobiles shiver with fear. Even with their headlights on they cannot see the road ahead. Train engineers back into stations after chugging past them in the blinding murk. In cities hundreds of miles away from the center of the dust storm, people shut their windows and doors and tape up the frames to keep out the invading dust. But a fog of dust fills the rooms relentlessly, settles slowly and silently, covering people and furniture and carpets in a thick, brownish gray blanket. Outside, bewildered hawks with bleak cries soar higher and higher into the blackened sky.

The dust storm travels as far as New York City. It sifts down onto ships hundreds of miles from the Atlantic coast. It began in the early 1930s. And it happened again, and again, and again. Drought settled

A farm boy tries to shield his mouth and nose from the dust storm devastating his family's land. Photo by Arthur Rothstein of the Farm Security Administration (FSA).

over the Southwest. And lasted, year after year after year. When would normal rains return? The farming regions of the Great Plains began to look like a wasteland. Would they ever again be fertile?

Farm families abandoned all hope of making a living on the land. They moved west, at first in a trickle, then in a flood. California! Land of promise! That was their goal, their hope of survival, their dream of prosperity. How could this happen? Why did it happen? What became of those hundreds of thousands who made the great migration to the West?

That is the story of this book.

A farm woman on the windswept plains of the Texas Panhandle, photographed by Dorothea Lange, 1938. Lange had a unique gift for catching a facial expression and a gesture to produce a portrait of great power.

One

A Dollar Down— and a Dollar Forever

THE DUST STORMS OF THE 1930S RANKED AMONG THE WORST ENVIRON-mental disasters in world history. They created a Dust Bowl containing more than one hundred counties in Kansas, Oklahoma, Colorado, New Mexico, and Texas. In one of the worst storms—the "black blizzard" of May 11, 1934—300 million tons of soil were blown away. The storms went on for seven long years. Years that were marked too by the Great Depression. It wasn't only the terrible weather that drove farmers to migrate west. It was also the hard times a vast number of Americans suffered in that decade.

Actually, for the farmer, the economic crisis of the thirties was but a new depression piled on top of an old one. The "Dust Bowlers" who streamed westward from the Great Plains and the South moved for caus-es more deep-rooted and enduring than the hardships caused by these extreme changes in the weather.

11

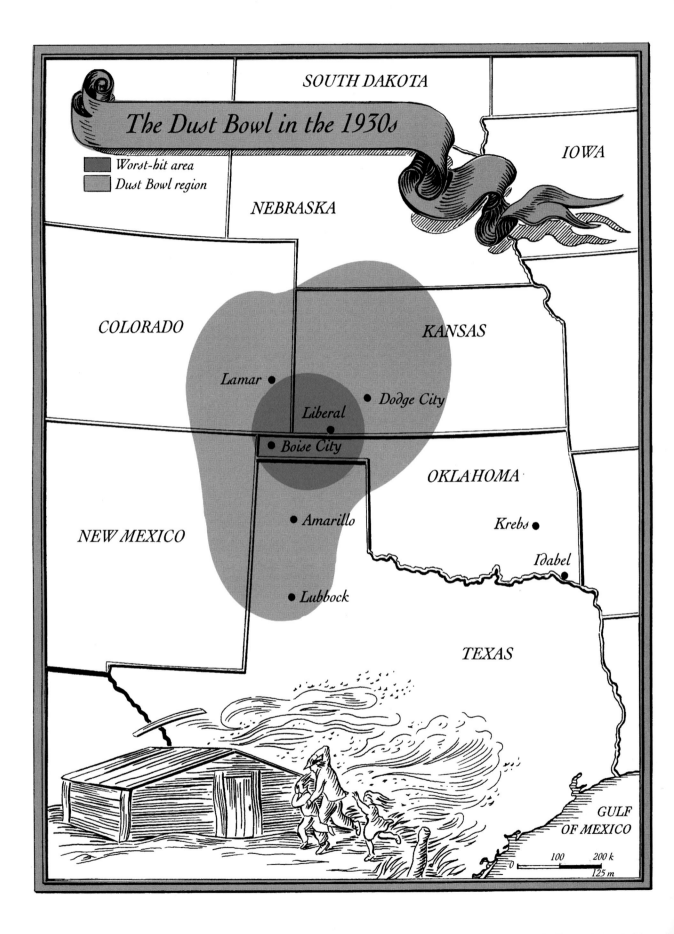

SOUTH DAKOTA

IOWA

The Dust Bowl in the 1930s

Worst-hit area
Dust Bowl region

NEBRASKA

COLORADO

KANSAS

Lamar •

• Dodge City

Liberal
•

• Boise City

OKLAHOMA

NEW MEXICO

• Amarillo

Krebs •

Idabel •

• Lubbock

TEXAS

GULF
OF MEXICO

0   100   200 k

125 m

Until World War I, the region that later became known as the Dust Bowl was grassland used mostly for grazing cattle. But with the increased demand for food from a Europe ravaged by war, and the resulting high prices, millions of acres were put under the plow to grow wheat.

Through a broad swath, starting in Kansas and running into Texas, farmers lured by quick profits plowed submarginal land. The native grazing land was soon gone. Gone too were its root systems, which held the soil in place. No one foresaw how this would come back to haunt the High Plains during the Dust Bowl.

As the 1920s came on, American farmers faced strong competition from the nations of Europe recovering from the devastation of World War I. The prices of farm products dropped as Europe returned to normal production. As a result, American farms sank into a depression from 1920 to 1921.

Farmers also faced problems caused by their own efficiency. Advances in farm technology led to the use of more tractors. A tractor could do a lot of work in a short time. You could use it all day, and even all night. Every tractor put at least a few farmhands out of work. Fewer people were needed to raise farm produce. Yet most of those surplus farmworkers could not find jobs elsewhere. They stayed on the land, often with only a few weeks of work at harvesttime, or none at all.

Machinery hit the small farmer hardest of all. He didn't operate on a scale large enough to afford tractors. He had to go. "Tractored out," he said. Some small farmers remained near home, trying to make a living on land not fit for farming. Others migrated in ever larger numbers to California.

Many farmers borrowed heavily during the war and postwar years to buy land at inflated prices and to buy costly machinery too. Their heavy debt would sink them when the Great Depression forced both the farm prices and land values way down.

It's worth noting here the powerful changes in farming brought

Submarginal land in Texas has been plowed under to grow wheat, foreshadowing the disaster to come. (Dorothea Lange)

about by that new mechanization. Farming before this had involved much self-sufficient food-raising. Farm families took care of milk cows and raised chickens and eggs, produce, and hogs and cattle for slaughter. They grew small cash crops of wheat and feed grains. But industrial farming soon took over, requiring large amounts of capital and equipment to produce ever larger crops with the sole aim of making higher and higher profits.

The empty home of a "tractored out" farmer in Hall County, Texas.

So things were not very good for the farmer in the 1920s. The "Roaring Twenties" people called these years, or the "Prosperous Twenties." In most people's minds the American dream of unlimited plenty seemed close to realization. The mass production of consumer goods had reached fantastic heights. From privy, icebox, and buggy the country moved almost overnight into a new era of bathroom, electric refrigerator, and automobile. Advertising stimulated the public to buy washing machines, vacuum cleaners, telephones, and lots of products people didn't need. From creating their own fun through parlor games, people turned to the radio and the movies. Press and politicians trumpeted the news that America was aboard an express train hurtling toward permanent prosperity.

On May 7, 1929, an advertiser planted this full-page announcement in the *New York Times*:

> You business executives sitting at your desks, you have been making a fairy tale come true. Within ten years you have done more toward the sum total of human happiness than has ever been done before in all the centuries of historical time.

As business profits soared, many felt the urge to get rich quickly. A speculative fever took hold as new investors gambled on the stock market. But not everyone had the extra funds to play with. A national survey of family incomes made in 1929 showed that of the country's 27.5 million families, 21.5 million, or 75 percent, were not doing so well. They earned under $3,000 a year ($60 a week). And among them were six million families with incomes under $1,000 a year ($20 a week).

Families with incomes below $3,000 could save nothing at all. No matter, said the salesmen—just buy on the installment plan. "A dollar down and a dollar forever." Personal debt piled higher and higher.

The gap between rich and poor was wide, and growing wider. The 27,500 wealthiest families had as much money as the 12 million poorest families. The nation's top and bottom were worlds apart. Down in Appalachian coal mines, up in Northwest lumber mills, men endured great hardship for ten dollars a week. This, while Henry Ford was rich

Christmas gifts advertised in household magazines promised a new era of enduring prosperity.

PRACTICAL GIFTS
That will delight any woman

Electric Table Lamp
$4.50

Electric Toaster
$4.00

ELECTRICAL devices for the home—things that make the duties lighter and the home brighter—these are the gifts most welcome. And they exemplify the true Christmas spirit— the spirit of doing good to others in the most practical manner.

Why not surprise your wife or mother with a Western Electric vacuum cleaner—a washing machine—a dish washer—an electric iron or an Inter-phone between bedroom and kitchen? All of these save much hard work and many steps. Or, why not give her the soothing comfort of a Western Electric warming pad, or the convenience of the toaster, or the beauty of the table lamp? These, and many more needfuls, comprise the list of

The Vacuum Cleaner not built like a broom.

American Beauty Electric Iron
$5.00

No. 11 Vacuum Cleaner
$32.50

Western Electric
Household Helps

They exemplify the high quality of all Western Electric merchandise, and are guaranteed by the world's largest distributors of electrical supplies. The Bell Telephone, which you use so often, is made by this company, and is an evidence of Western Electric worth.

This is the "Push-a-Button Age," in which the well-equipped housewife has electricity's power at her beck and call. Electricity is a willing helper, and the cost of current to operate any of these household helps is surprisingly low.

Electric Warming Pad
$6.50
The successor to the hot-water bag.

Two Inter-phones Complete with Material for Installing $15.00

Electrical dealers all over the country sell our goods. Write to any of our houses in the cities listed below, and we will send you our booklet, "An Electrical Christmas," and tell you where in your vicinity our goods may be purchased. Ask for Booklet No. 61-T.

WESTERN ELECTRIC COMPANY
Manufacturers of the 8,000,000 "Bell" Telephones

Electric Dish Washer

New York	Chicago	Kansas City	San Francisco	Montreal
Buffalo	Milwaukee	St. Louis	Salt Lake City	Portland
Philadelphia	Pittsburgh	Oklahoma City	Oakland	Toronto
Boston	Cleveland	Minneapolis	Los Angeles	Winnipeg
Richmond	Detroit	St. Paul	Dallas	Calgary
Atlanta	Cincinnati	Denver	Houston	Vancouver
Savannah	Indianapolis	Omaha	Seattle	Edmonton
New Orleans				

EQUIPMENT FOR EVERY ELECTRICAL NEED

Electric Washing Machine

Two raggedy boys, one shoeless, in the back of their rickety family wagon as it heads out for a Texas cotton field. The earnings of the entire family were not enough to lift them from the bottom rung of the economic ladder.

Long before the Great Depression set in, millions of Americans knew hard times. This coal-mining family lived in a tiny, decrepit shack, surrounded by barren land. Adequate food and medical care were beyond their reach. The baby in the mother's arms, who looks a few months old, is actually a year old.

enough to pay for just one year a tax of $2,609,000, and John D. Rockefeller Jr., $6,278,000.

During the 1920s the goal of all the presidents—Harding, Coolidge, and Hoover—was to cut government spending and reduce taxes. In 1928, even as the biggest capital investors were carried to new peaks of wealth, the government chopped the income tax of the very rich. By 1929 the 5 percent of Americans with the highest income were taking in about one-third of all personal income.

How were working people doing? Did they have good steady jobs? Were they ever laid off? The answer wasn't easy to come by. The government before the mid-1930s hadn't much interest in such questions. But enough hard data exists to show that in the second half of the twenties the number of workers temporarily laid off averaged 14 percent. In 1928, said Senator Robert F. Wagner of New York, the number of unemployed reached 5.8 million. And the Great Depression would not begin for another year.

Look into almost any corner of the country and you'd find people in trouble. The Allegheny coal towns, the textile centers of New England, the tenants and croppers of the Deep South, the shipbuilding and shoe-manufacturing cities of the North—they suffered hard times all through the twenties. So did farmers almost everywhere. Prices of farm produce slipped badly after World War I, as we have seen, and had not made their way up again.

Dorothea Lange, a successful photographer of San Francisco's upper class, stopped doing commercial studio work in 1932, as the Depression left 14 million people without jobs. She shot this picture of an unshaven, hunched-up man in a battered hat, leaning on a railing with an empty tin cup between his arms. His hands are clenched, the line of his mouth is bitter, while behind him others wait for a handout. "White Angel Bread Line" became one of the great images of the Depression.

Two

Breadlines and Shantytowns

ON A LATE OCTOBER DAY IN 1929 THERE WAS A SEVERE BREAK IN STOCK market prices. Wall Street brokers felt jittery, anxious about what might happen. The next day prices plunged sickeningly. They fell faster and faster that morning, and by 11 o'clock it was like an avalanche. Panic seized the market. Wild rumors swept speculators, big and little. Losses were tremendous, day after day. The panic went on smashing prices. By mid-November $30 billion had blown away—the same amount of money America had spent on World War I. Overnight the life savings of many went down the drain.

But President Hoover reassured the nation. Everything was "on a sound and prosperous basis," he said, adding that any lack of confidence in the future was "foolish."

He was wrong. The Great Depression had begun.

How did it happen?

No student of that era believes there was any single cause of it. The economists think it was a combination of several factors. The most basic seem to be these:

During the postwar boom years industry built more and bigger plants. Soon they were able to produce far more than they could sell.

Business had kept prices and profits high. As monopolies developed they were able to control prices, keeping them high so as to make still more profit. At the same time, with labor unions nonexistent or weak, they were able to keep wages low. That meant labor didn't get enough pay to buy back its share of what it had produced.

With improved technology, more goods could be produced by fewer workers. Labor-saving machines began putting more and more people out of work in industry after industry. When fewer people are employed, less money is paid out in wages. So there is less money to buy the goods coming off production lines.

Farmers had been in a bad way since World War I, when they produced more than ever before to feed and clothe the armed forces and the peoples of Europe. After the war, even though Europe's farmers were back at work, American farmers kept up high levels of production. Of course surpluses piled up. And with supply greater than demand, farmers were forced to accept lower prices. That meant they had too little income to buy what the factories were turning out.

Credit was so easy to get during the twenties that a great many people went deep into debt as they bought on the installment plan or ventured into new businesses. People poured their profits (or borrowed money to do it) into the stock market, even at high prices, gambling on the hope that they would be able to sell at even higher prices. Soon stock prices were far above the real value of businesses. The balloon inflated more and more. When it finally burst, stockholders rushed to sell, fearing prices would drop even farther. And so they did.

All these weaknesses underlay our complicated economic system. No

Only days after the stock market crash in October 1929, this speculator had to put his new roadster up for sale.

aspect of it was regulated by the government. It was a free-for-all. So any part of the system could be thrown wildly off balance. When the panic hit Wall Street that fall of 1929, it was like the breaking of a dam that releases devastating floodwaters.

Within two months several million people lost their jobs. Many businesses closed their doors. Factories cut down on production, laid off workers, and reduced orders to suppliers. Salespeople were let go from stores. Recently completed office buildings, apartment houses, and hotels hunted in vain for tenants. Construction came to a dead halt. Cities opened up free employment bureaus to help people find work. Whether you were a skilled mechanic or a boy of seventeen, any job at all would do. But where were the jobs? A new song was heard: "I Don't Want Your Millions, Mister." The words went:

> I don't want your millions, mister
> I don't want your diamond ring,
> All I want is the right to live, mister;
> Give me back my job again.
> I don't want your Rolls-Royce, mister,
> I don't want your pleasure yacht.
> All I want is food for my babies;
> Give me my old job back.
> Think me dumb if you wish, mister,
> Call me green, or blue, or red.
> This one thing I sure know, mister:
> My hungry babies must be fed.
> We worked to build this country, mister,
> While you enjoyed a life of ease.
> You've stolen all that we built, mister;
> Now our children starve and freeze.

Bank after bank failed. By the fall of 1932 over six thousand of them—about one out of four in the country—had closed their doors. Nine million people who believed their savings had been safely stored deep within steel vaults saw their cash disappear overnight. The shock left them thinking there was nothing, nothing anymore they could believe in.

People with their jobs gone, their savings gone, and maybe only a small life insurance policy left, suddenly realized that for the first time in their life they were worth more dead than alive.

FSA photographers gave the country glimpses of people in trouble. At left, a lumberman in Minnesota (by Russell Lee); at right, farm children (by Carl Mydans).

1930, 1931, 1932—three years of increasing unemployment and of hand-to-mouth relief. City after city trying to feed a half or a third or a quarter of its citizens upon shrunken taxes or charitable donations.

In September 1932 *Fortune* magazine reported:

City after city maintaining the lives but not the health of the unemployed on a survival ration; city after city where the whole mechanism of relief has failed or is about to fail or has survived only by abandoning a major part of its task; and beyond the cities the mill towns and the coal mines and the 'cropper farms where relief is merely a name.

By the spring of 1930 lines of homeless men seeking shelter snaked through the streets of every American city. A shelter opened by New York City's welfare department took in 1,100 men in a night. They were allowed to sleep there only five nights in one month. A year later a volunteers' census of the homeless counted 15,000 with no shelter, no prospect of a job, and no place to stay in the daytime or to sleep at night.

Unemployment became a way of life. And out of it came a new kind of housing. The jobless began to create their own shelters wherever they could find unused land—in vacant lots, in swamps, under bridges, beside railroad tracks. The shantytowns were made of tin and packing boxes, strips of cardboard, old tar paper, waste lumber—anything that could be foraged. In New York City such shacks were strung along for two miles between Riverside Drive and the Hudson River. "Hoovervilles," these communities were called, in honor of the thrifty president.

One of New York's largest squatter colonies was on the bank of the Hudson River, at 74th Street and Riverside Drive. By contrast, one of the largest private homes was just across the drive from the Hooverville. It was the $8 million palace of Charles M. Schwab, the retired steel king, who took over an entire block to be comfortable. His home had seventy-five rooms, forty baths, a marble swimming pool, a gymnasium, a billiard room with ten tables, a bowling alley, a mahogany wine closet, and a private chapel. In 1934 the city forced the homeless to break up their Hooverville and move out. To go where? No one knew. But now Schwab had an unobstructed view of the beautiful Hudson.

A sight new to the country was the army of young people on the road. By late 1932 a quarter of a million teenagers were roaming the

Within a few months, breadlines like this one on Manhattan's Bowery laced the streets of many cities.

Separately or in organized groups the unemployed protested their conditions. Here a father uses his two children to appeal for funds while placing the blame on President Hoover.

country. Freight trains swarmed with kids whose families couldn't feed them anymore, or whose homes had broken up. They bummed their food, lived in hobo jungles or empty boxcars. Many had been to high school, some even to college, graduating into long years of morale-wrecking unemployment.

"Man Beside Wheelbarrow," a photo by Dorothea Lange, 1934. The slumped body, the overturned barrow, and the harsh, blank wall all convey the emotion of hopelessness.

Three

One Cent for
One Farm

BY THE WINTER OF 1932–1933 THE JOBLESS NUMBERED EIGHT MILLION, one in six of the working population. Most cities had laws to prevent married women from working in local government. If women teachers married, they were fired by most school systems. Yet often during those hard times the women were the sole breadwinners of their families.

How to solve the crisis? President Hoover offered optimism, cheerfulness, hope. "Spread the work," he advised business. When some suggested the government should create public works to provide jobs, he answered, "No, federal funding wouldn't be wise."

The government had some 60 million bushels of wheat in storage. Distribute it to the hungry? "No," said Hoover, though feed was supplied to farmers to keep cattle alive. "How come there are so many men and women out on the street selling apples?" people asked. "Well," replied Hoover, "many people left their jobs for the more profitable one of selling apples."

A congressman on his way from the Capitol in 1930, where nothing has been done to help the Depression's victims, stops to buy an apple from an unemployed man. How far will a nickel go to restore a person's dignity?

It is hard to blame Hoover or anyone else for their blindness to the depth of the crisis. To predict what would come was almost impossible, for nothing of this extent and duration had ever happened before. Just about every country in the world, and every part of the economy, felt the Depression's devastating blows. The number of people thrown out of work was greater than ever before. Unemployment was the central problem of that agonizing decade.

The reach of the crisis was by no means limited to the cities. Farmers who owned their land, tenants, sharecroppers, hired hands—all suffered from the pathetically low prices they got for their products. Whether you were a fruit rancher in California, a dairy farmer in upstate New York, a cotton grower in Mississippi, or a corn and hog farmer in Iowa, you suffered. You felt yourself lucky if you could sell your goods for just about what it cost you to produce them.

Both the farmer and the city worker were ground down in poverty. The difference was that the jobless autoworker had nothing else to do. The farmer, however, continued to work as long and as hard as he ever did. A Carolina millhand had no capital to lose, while the farmer often lost all or most of his capital—land, tools, machinery, livestock, even household goods. And then the people he was deep in debt to would evict the family. Yet farmers might manage to raise some food for their own family at least, while the city people could not. They had to look to miserably inadequate local relief to survive. There were many cases of severe malnutrition, and of starvation too.

What did going without work for a long period of time do to people? Of course, they reacted in different ways. But nearly every study of the psychological effects of unemployment and poverty shows the same basic pattern:

When workers lost their job, they waited a while for something to turn up. But soon they began to hunt feverishly for a new job. If nothing came up, they were discouraged, often emotionally upset. If months

In southeastern Iowa, a tenant farmer's children at their dinner on Christmas day, 1936, as photographed by Russell Lee.

passed with nothing to do, many sank into apathy. They wondered, What's wrong with me? Am I good for nothing? Does my family think I'm worthless? Hopelessness could lead to failure to take any step to change the situation. Some learned to accept their very limited lives. Others lost their pride and avoided contact with other people. A broken spirit could mean gloom and bitterness, and lead to heavy drinking and outbursts of irrational rage. What made matters worse was the old American tradition of self-reliance. You were expected to make it on your own. Get hold of the ladder of success, and anyone could climb to the top, where there was room for all. It was simply up to you. So when you found yourself knocked off the ladder (through no fault of your own), and unable even to supply the bare necessities of life, it was a terrible and humiliating shock.

The mood of that time is captured in this passage by the reporter Richard Boer:

There was no rallying of forces or coming together to care for the sick and hungry although their number, increasing daily, was far greater than those injured or made homeless by tornado or earthquake. At first each man was alone, often sitting silently in his home, hiding his unemployment and growing poverty as if it were a shameful disease. Unlike a hurricane, the ravages of the depression could not be seen clearly in a well-defined path of destruction. Instead it was everywhere, and for a long time things looked almost as usual. But behind the cold, expressionless fronts of tenements, houses and apartments, inside and concealed from the public gaze, men and women struggled alone at first, viewing their plight as personal, private disasters, a slow and dreadful panic rising within them.

For the farmer, depression was nothing new. He had never shared in the limited prosperity of the 1920s. (A U.S. senator told the country that in 1929, 500 multimillionaires made more money than the combined income of 2,300,000 farmers raising wheat and cotton.) As the even leaner years came on, some down-and-out farmers quit the countryside to search for factory jobs. Very few found any. A vast amount of farm

In Georgia, an old cotton grower despairs of ever getting his heavily mortgaged farm out of debt. (Dorothea Lange)

produce went to waste because there was no profitable market, while millions of the unemployed hungered for food.

Oscar Ameringer, a newspaper editor, roamed the country for three months observing poverty amid plenty. He told a congressional committee in February 1932 what he saw:

The last thing I saw on the night I left Seattle was numbers of women searching for scraps of food in the refuse piles of the principal markets of that city. A number of Montana citizens told me of thousands of bushels of wheat left in the fields uncut on account of the low price that hardly paid for the harvesting. In Oregon I saw thousands of bushels of apples rotting in the orchards. At the same time there are millions of children who, on account of the poverty of their parents, will not eat one apple this winter.

In Oregon, thousands of ewes were killed by the sheep raisers because they did not bring enough on the market to pay the freight on them. And while Oregon sheep raisers fed mutton to the buzzards, I saw men picking for meat scraps in the garbage cans of New York and Chicago.

The roads of the West and Southwest teem with hungry hitchhikers. The campfires of the homeless are seen along every railroad track. I saw men, women and children walking over the hard roads. Most of them were tenant farmers who had lost their all in the late slump in wheat and cotton.

In Oklahoma, Texas, Arkansas and Louisiana I saw untold bales of cotton rotting in the fields because the cotton pickers could not keep body and soul together on 35 cents paid for picking 100 pounds. The farmers are being pauperized by the poverty of industrial populations and the industrial populations are being pauperized by the farmers. Neither has the money to buy the product of the other, hence we have overproduction and underconsumption at the same time and in the same country.

With city food prices too low for farmers to cover their production costs, many took militant action to block nonstrikers from delivering their goods. Above, strikers near Sioux City, Iowa, stop milk trucks from entering the city. At right, using tear gas and clubs, police chase striking pecan workers near San Antonio, Texas.

No wonder the nation's farmers became angry and militant. Thousands of them went on strike against prices so low that crops were being sold for less than cost. The farmers of Iowa, Illinois, North Dakota, Nebraska, and New York grabbed pitchforks and monkey wrenches, set up roadblocks and barricades on the highways that led to markets. They were following the old advice of the Populists of the 1890s: "Raise less corn and more hell!" Stones crashed through the windshields of farmers who tried to run the blockade and sell their produce. Milk was dumped, trucks were wrecked, their drivers beaten, vegetables and grain scattered to the roadside.

A farmers' organization sprang up, trying to raise farm prices by

stopping the shipment of food into the cities until prices went up. They proclaimed their demands:

We have issued an ultimatum to the other groups of society. If you continue to confiscate our property and demand that we feed your stomachs and clothe your bodies we will refuse to function. We don't ask people to make implements, cloth, or houses at the price of degradation, bankruptcy, dissolution, and despair.

Farmers had already mortgaged their land to the hilt by the time the Great Depression began—$9.5 billion—the outcome of a ten-year depres-

Neighbors gather when a farmer's property is auctioned off because he cannot meet his mortgage payments. Their silent presence is a threat against anyone who dares bid.

sion among farmers. And all the while their taxes had been rising, more than 250 percent in the 1920s. In Virginia, in just one day, hundreds of farmers were evicted for nonpayment of taxes. Between 1930 and 1935 about 750,000 farms were lost through foreclosure and bankruptcy sales.

As reports of mortgage sales—for failure to meet monthly payments and interest—poured in, farmers felt threatened with the loss of all they had. Enraged, many joined together in local resistance movements. When a sale was announced, people were warned that anyone buying that farm wouldn't find life worth living there. Auctioneers fearing for their safety would go through the make-believe of asking for bids: "Ten dollars!" "Five dollars!" "One cent!" would be cried out from the crowd . . . and the farm would go back to its owner. His livelihood had been saved, for the time being.

But nothing—no act of man or government—could halt the even graver threat to farm security: the dust storms.

The wreckage symbolizes the havoc caused by a 1933 dust storm in the West. (Arthur Rothstein)

Four

A Stricken Land

In the southwest corner of Kansas, 109 people, members of 26 families, left their homes in the spring of 1935, all of them driven out by drought and dust storms. Most had lived there for over ten years, some as long as forty years. Two neighbors had died of dust pneumonia, and others were sick with it.

That June in Oklahoma, a woman wrote her friends to describe her family's battle with dust storms:

Wearing our shade hats, with handkerchiefs tied over our faces and vaseline in our nostrils, we have been trying to rescue our home from the accumulations of wind-blown dust which penetrates wherever air can go. It is an almost hopeless task, for there is rarely a day when at some time the dust clouds do not roll over. "Visibility" approaches zero and everything is covered again with

43

a silt-like deposit which may vary in depth from a film to actual ripples on the kitchen floor. I keep oiled cloths on the window sills and between the upper and lower sashes. They help just a little to retard or collect the dust. Some seal the windows with the gummed-paper strips used in wrapping parcels, but no method is fully effective. We buy what appears to be red cedar sawdust with oil added to use in sweeping our floors, and do our best to avoid inhaling the irritating dust.

There was no more grass or even weeds on her 640-acre farm than on her friend's kitchen floor, she added. While on a sixty-mile trip to have a tractor repaired, she reported:

We saw many pitiful reminders of broken homes and apparently wasted effort. Little abandoned homes where people had drilled deep wells for the precious water, had set trees and vines, built reservoirs, and fenced in gardens,—with everything now walled in or half buried by the banks of drifted soil,—told a painful story of loss and disappointment. I grieved especially over one lonely plum thicket buried to the tips of the twigs, and a garden with a fence closely built of boards for wind protection, now enclosing only a hillock of dust covered with the blue-flowered bull nettles which no winds or sands discourage.

This was the fourth successive year of drought and crop failure throughout a great part of the plains region. In June there were two most welcome rains. But less than an inch fell each time. Any help the rain might have been, she said, was . . .

. . . largely destroyed by the drifting soil from abandoned, unworked lands around. It fills the air and our eyes and noses and throats, and, worst of all, our furrows, where tender shoots are coming to

Three men are caught outdoors in the Kansas wheat belt when a dust storm suddenly sweeps in. The blizzard of dirt threatens to blow them off their feet.

the surface only to be buried by the smothering silt from the fields of rugged individualists who persist in their right to do nothing.

A fairly promising piece of barley has been destroyed for us by the merciless drift from the same field whose sands have practically buried the little mulberry hedge which has long sheltered our buildings from the northwest winds. Large spaces in our pastures are entirely bare in spite of the rains. Most of the green color, where there is any grazing, is due to the pestilent Russian thistles rather than to grass. Our little locust grove which we cherished for so many years has become a small pile of fence posts. With trees and vines and flowers all around you, you can't imagine how I miss that little green shaded spot in the midst of the desert glare.

Why didn't that family pick up and leave as so many had done? She explains her reasons:

I cannot act or feel or think as if the experiences of our twenty-seven years of life together had never been. And they are all bound up with the little corner to which we have given our continued and united efforts. To leave voluntarily—to break all these closely knit ties for the sake of a possibly greater comfort elsewhere—seems like defaulting on our task. We may have to leave. We can't hold out indefinitely without some return from the land, some source of income, however small. But I think I can never go willingly or without pain that as yet seem unendurable.

As she finished her letter, she wrote, "A great reddish-brown dust cloud is rising now from the southeast. . . ."

Oklahoma was the most windblown state in the country. Its newly broken red plains were among the worst eroded. Dust was not new on the Great Plains. But never had it been so destructive as in the thirties. Paul Taylor, professor of economics at the University of California, Berkeley, explains why:

Dried by years of drought and pulverized by machine-drawn gang disk plows, the soil was literally thrown to the winds, which whipped it in clouds across the country. The winds churned the soil, leaving vast stretches of farms blown and hummocked like deserts or the margins of beaches. They loosened the hold of settlers on the land, and like particles of dust drove them rolling down ribbons of highway.

Writing of a great dust storm in 1934, Russell Lord described its far reach:

A woman of the Great Plains, staring out of her farmhouse door at the bleak eroded land. (Dorothea Lange)

Gently sifted with a nice precision the finest part of our Plains soil fell upon boat decks and waves of the Atlantic far at sea. . . . In Texas, the skim milk—sand; in the midland, median particles; in Ohio, a light, unseen deposit, soon whisked away by water; and overhead, in Maryland the very cream of rich far-western soils blowing out to sea to be drowned and lost.

The first great dust storm to hit South Dakota came in 1933. The Karnstrum farm of 470 acres in Beadle County experienced it early on the morning of November 11. The family told a magazine reporter what happened:

By mid-morning a gale was blowing, cold and black. By noon it was blacker than night, because one can see through night and this was an opaque black. It was a wall of dirt one's eyes could not penetrate, but it could penetrate the eyes and ears and nose. It could penetrate to the lungs until one coughed up black. If a person was outside, he tied his handkerchief around his face, but he still coughed up black; and inside the house the Karnstrums soaked sheets and towels and stuffed them around the window ledges, but these didn't help much.

They were afraid because they had never seen anything like this before.

When the wind died and the sun shone forth again, it was on a different world. There were no fields, only sand drifting into mounds and eddies that swirled in what was now but an autumn breeze. There was no longer a section-line road 50 feet from the front door. It was obliterated. In the farmyard, fences, machinery, and trees were gone, buried. The roofs of sheds stuck out through drifts deeper than a man is tall.

It was only noon, but when a dust storm was blowing on the Colorado highway, to a frightened driver it felt like blackest midnight.

The amount of farmland ruined in that decade was enormous. There are about 423 million arable acres of cropland in the entire country. In 1934, according to a federal agency's report, 35 million acres were totally destroyed for farming. And almost all the topsoil of another 125 million acres was eroded. On another 100 million acres, serious damage was in progress.

Exactly what happened to the soil in the Dust Bowl when a powerful wind blew up? The historian Paul Bonnifield tells us:

On a small corner of the leeward side of a field, a particle of soil, broken loose by the wind, struck a cluster of soil particles like a cue

A farmer and his sons flee a dust storm in Oklahoma. (Arthur Rothstein)

ball striking the racked balls. The avalanching effect of soil erosion gathered force as it moved across the field. By the time the effects of one tiny wind-driven soil particle reached the opposite side of the field, a mighty force was assembled to assault the neighboring abandoned field. Soon a dirt storm was burning any living plant, while the soil around the plant's roots was joining the race across the stricken land.

James R. Dickenson, a Washington correspondent raised in Kansas, experienced first-hand as a boy what drought and dust did to the people of his state in the thirties:

The dust and drought went on day in, day out, week in, week out, interminably and almost unbearably, parching the land and burning out pastures and crops, with the wind stripping the topsoil in some parts of a field, and blowing it into dunes in others. Many areas lost as much as five or six inches of topsoil and much was stripped to the hardpan. Farmers helplessly watched their livestock die of thirst and starvation and many were forced to sell their herds at a loss in a glutted market. Many cattle died from ingesting dirt as they rooted for forage, and the dirt in their feed wore their teeth down to the gums. . . .

Drought and depression parched people's souls and blasted their hopes, in some cases permanently. "It wasn't unusual for people to just get up and walk away from their homes, furniture and everything, particularly since many were renting," Aunt Opal recalled. I remember my uncles expressing the wish that weeds would grow in the fields simply to help keep them from blowing away.

Dickenson told of other dangers living in the Dust Bowl. There was the time when a group of teenage boys were out hunting for arrowheads

Cattle were among the victims hardest hit by the 1930s drought. Their tongues swelled in parched mouths, their legs wobbly from weakness, their bones visible through shrunken hide, they were put out of their misery by government marksmen.

and were caught in a storm. Finally, when the dust settled, the boys found their way home. People learned to get down and stay down whenever a storm blew up. If you couldn't find a fence line to follow, it was likely you'd get lost.

Dust that clogged the lungs, windpipe, and intestines caused pneumonia, and people of all ages died of it. Silicosis, a disease common to miners, took lives too.

Dickenson recalled the terror of living through a storm:

On one blindingly sunny, scalding summer afternoon in 1935 or 1936, three of my cousins and I were playing under the trees that shaded the livestock watering tank on Uncle Vernie's farm north of Rolla when one of those black monsters peeped over the northwest horizon and was soon bearing down on us like an express train. When we spotted it, we began the panicky race across the farmyard, a trek made difficult by the fact that the hot sandy soil burned our bare feet. Shortly after we reached the house, the storm hit and bright afternoon turned pitch black.

Uncle Vernie had been running his John Deere tractor in the field just east of the farm buildings. When he saw the storm coming, he unhitched his implement and made his own race for home on the tractor. He lost. When the storm struck and plunged his universe into sudden, total blackness, he couldn't see the front end of the tractor. He had made it into the barnyard, however, and ran the tractor into one of the trees by the stock tank, where we had been playing a few minutes before. This, on a farm that was his home for fifty years. The tank gave him an orientation point and he was able to follow the fence to the house, which in such storms was like a fort under siege.

Coming on top of the Depression, the great dust storms of the early thirties completed the ruin of hundreds of thousands of farmers. Their land had blown away. It was no longer theirs. The farms and homes their forebears had shaped out of wilderness had returned to wilderness.

So they loaded the family and a few belongings into an old truck or jalopy. And headed west.

A homeless family of four, tractored out in Childress County, Texas, 1938. (Dorothea Lange)

Five

Okies

ANY DAY, ALONG THE HIGHWAYS OF THE SOUTHWEST, YOU COULD SEE hungry and bewildered men and women trundling handcarts and baby carriages piled high with shabby household goods, their children trudging behind. Rattling slowly by them were battered old cars loaded with bedding and cooking utensils and children, with suitcases and sacks strapped to the running boards.

Along U.S. Highway 30 they walked or drove through the Idaho hills, along Route 66 across New Mexico and Arizona, along the Old Spanish Trails through El Paso, along all the other westward roads. In a single hour an observer watching beside an Idaho road counted thirty-four autos with license plates of states between Chicago and the Rocky Mountains. They were part of a vast migratory movement. Wrote the historian Frederick Lewis Allen:

Carts, wagons, and jalopies piled high with the belongings of Dust Bowl refugees straggled west along the highways. Where to? What next?

When they camped by the wayside they might find themselves next to a family of evicted white Alabama sharecroppers who had been on the move for four years, snatching seasonal farm labor jobs wherever they could through the Southwest; or next to tenant families from the Arkansas Delta who had been "tractored off"

their land—expelled in order that the owner might consolidate two or three farms and operate them with tractors and day labor; or next to lone wanderers who had once held industrial jobs and had now for years been on relief or on the road—jumping freights, hitchhiking, panhandling, shunting back and forth across the countryside in the faint hope of a durable job.

About one million people took to the road during the worst years of the Depression. Many were refugees from the Dust Bowl, the families of homesteading pioneers who had at last given up their struggle to make a living on the land. These were the "removal" migrants, forced into migratory life by loss of land or a job. For other migrants, following the crops seasonally was an habitual way of life, which they would go on doing year after year until they were too old to work.

The best-known migrants of the Great Depression were the "Okies" made famous by the novelist John Steinbeck. (He would win the Nobel Prize in literature for *The Grapes of Wrath*.) Highway 66 was the route Steinbeck's fictional family, the Joads, traveled. Back in the thirties it was just two lanes of concrete twisting its way through dozens of crowded main streets and over dozens of railroad crossings. Nothing more than a lot of little roads patched with detours, and yet they called it a national highway.

One of the great photographers of migrant life was Dorothea Lange. Beginning in 1934 she joined her husband, economist Paul Taylor, in extensive field research into the conditions and needs of the Dust Bowlers fleeing west. Taylor's reports combined with Lange's photos were strongly influential in launching federal programs to alleviate the plight of the dispossessed farmers.

In the field, Lange would talk with the people she photographed, and then immediately afterwards make notes on what they said. In these excerpts from her notes you can hear their voices:

We ain't no paupers. We hold ourselves to be decent folks. We don't want no relief. But what we do want is a chanst to make an honest living like what we was raised.
A human being has a right to stand like a tree has a right to stand.
All we got to start with is a family of kids.
Yessir, we're starved, stalled and stranded.

Photographer Dorothea Lange perches atop a car for a better perspective. Photo taken by her husband and collaborator, Professor Paul Taylor.

I wouldn't have relief no way it was fixed.

I've wrote back that we're well and such as that, but I never have wrote that we live in a tent.

When you gits down to your last bean, your backbone and your navel shakes dice to see which gits it.

Brother, hit's pick seventy-five cent cotton or starve.

Dorothea Lange took this photograph in March 1936 at a pea pickers camp near Nipomo, California. She called it "Migrant Mother." One of five exposures of the mother and her children, this image would be reproduced innumerable times in books, magazines, newspapers, pamphlets, and films and would be shown worldwide in exhibitions and on television. It is regarded as one of the great American photographs.

If I could get me a piece of land I'd go to diggin' it with my hands.
A piece of meat in the house would like to scare these children of
mine to death.
Us people has got to stick together to get by these hard times.

When the migrants finally straggled into California they quickly
found it was no golden land. Not for the poor, not for the landless. Here
is a farmer from Texas with six kids whom Lange photographed in
Wasco, California. It is June 1938:

People just can't make it back there, with drought, hailstorms,
windstorms, duststorms, insects. People exist here and they can't
do that there. You can make it here if you sleep lots and eat little,
but it's pretty tough, there are so many people. They chase them
out of one camp because they say it isn't sanitary—there's no running water—so people live out here in the brush like a den o' dogs
or pigs.

In one squatter camp near Edison, on April 18, 1938, Taylor and
Lange counted 150 families at the potato sheds. Their auto license plates
showed they came from Minnesota, Missouri, Oklahoma, Arizona,
Arkansas, Texas, Nevada, Mississippi, Utah, New Mexico, Oregon, and
Washington.

Technology continued to change the way crops were planted and
harvested, eliminating jobs and reducing animal power. Shooting pic-
tures in the Imperial Valley in February 1939, Lange heard one migrant
worker say:

A machine to tie the carrots? They're fixin' to free all us fellows—
free us for what? Free us like they freed the mules. They're aimin'
at making slaves of us. We've got no more chance than a one-
legged man in a foot-race.

Goin' Down the Road

Perhaps nothing touches the heart more than the music that came out of the Great Depression. "Goin' Down the Road"—no one knows who wrote it—voices both the despair and the defiance of people struggling to survive those hard times. Folk singers like Woody Guthrie and Pete Seeger helped carry the music into every corner of the land.

I'm go - in' down the road feel - in' bad,_____
_ I'm_ go - in' down the road feel - in'
bad,_____ I'm go - in' down the
road feel - in' bad, Lord, Lord,__ And I
ain't gon - na be treat - ed this - a - way._____

I'm goin' where the dust storms never blow,
I'm goin' where the dust storms never blow,
I'm goin' where the dust storms never blow, Lord, Lord,
And I ain't gonna be treated thisaway.

I'm lookin' for a job with honest pay,
I'm lookin' for a job with honest pay,
I'm lookin' for a job with honest pay, Lord, Lord,
And I ain't gonna be treated thisaway.

Two dollar shoes hurt my feet,
Two dollar shoes hurt my feet,
Two dollar shoes hurt my feet, Lord, Lord,
And I ain't gonna be treated thisaway.

But ten dollar shoes fit 'em neat,
But ten dollar shoes fit 'em neat,
But ten dollar shoes fit 'em neat, Lord, Lord,
And I ain't gonna be treated thisaway.

I'm goin' where the water tastes like wine,
I'm goin' where the water tastes like wine,
I'm goin' where the water tastes like wine, Lord, Lord,
And I ain't gonna be treated thisaway.

Forty cents an hour won't pay my rent,
Forty cents an hour won't pay my rent,
Forty cents an hour won't pay my rent, Lord, Lord,
And I ain't gonna be treated thisaway.

I can't live on cornbread and beans,
I can't live on cornbread and beans,
I can't live on cornbread and beans, Lord, Lord,
And I ain't gonna be treated thisaway.

I'm goin' down the road feelin' bad,
I'm goin' down the road feelin' bad,
I'm goin' down the road feelin' bad, Lord, Lord,
And I ain't gonna be treated thisaway.

Children at an auto camp in Kern County, California. Their young parents have left the Texas Dust Bowl in search of work. Now the couple travels daily thirty-five miles to pick peas and thirty-five miles back. Working five hours each, together they earn $2.25. (Dorothea Lange)

Six

You Call This Living?

Were the Dust Bowl migrants needed in California? Agriculture in that state had become highly intensive. Demands for hand labor in peak season ran far above the local supply. But at other times of the year there were two or three migrants for every job. Most migrants had work for only about four to six months a year. Their average income—*per family*—was between $350 and $450 a year. Since they had to be on the move so often, out of that meager amount came the cost of gas, oil, and repairs for their old cars. The average migrant family contained four people. How much money was left to meet their basic needs for food, clothing, housing, medicine?

The farms they worked on were run like big food factories. Most owners were not on the spot; they operated out of sleek offices in the city. They hired local managers to supervise the workers. In California less than one-tenth of the farms produced over one-half of the crops.

"Stoop labor" they called it. Migrant workers endured long hours in the harvest season, bent over almost double, for wages that did not bring them a decent living.

Look at just one such food factory, near the town of Delano. It was owned by the DiGiorgio family. On the company's nine thousand acres, diverse crops were raised—melons, eggplants, grapes, raisins, peas, almonds, prunes, onions, potatoes, peaches, cotton. In peak season their farms gave hourly work to 1,800 people.

The DiGiorgios supplied housing, of a kind. Labor camps for single men were segregated by race and nationality—Japanese, Filipino,

Mexican, and "American," meaning white. No matter what kind of work the migrants did, rates were set so that the pay usually came to $2.50 a day.

How did the Dust Bowlers live? Near Modesto, a town in the San Joaquin Valley, you could see how they tried to improve their living conditions as best they could. First, it was a tent or trailer parked on a lot. Then a lean-to shack at the rear of the lot. And finally a little one- or two-room frame shack they built themselves. Often all the people in such a place came from the same county or small town back home.

Most such families were on relief for part of the year or worked on jobs created by the Works Progress Administration (WPA), a federal work relief agency. There just wasn't enough fieldwork to make a living. The quality of their living ranged from tolerable to terribly bad. An example of the worst is the ditch-bank or roadside squatter camp. The state occasionally sent out investigators to check on migrant living conditions. One of the reports, made in 1936, said:

In Imperial County, many families were found camping out by the side of irrigation ditches, with little or no shelter. One such family consisted of the father, mother, and eight children. The father hoped there would be some work in the valley later in the year. The mother had tuberculosis and pellagra. . . . One of the children had active tuberculosis. The family had no home but a 1921 Ford. The mother was trying to chop some wood for the fire. . . . A meat and vegetable stew was being cooked in a large, rusty tin can over a grate supported by four other cans. A cupboard and a table had been constructed of boxes. There were no toilet facilities, Nature's needs being attended to behind bushes. Some water was brought from the ice plant in El Centro for drinking purposes, but for cooking and washing, water from the irrigation ditches was used. The family had been sleeping on the ground. The blankets

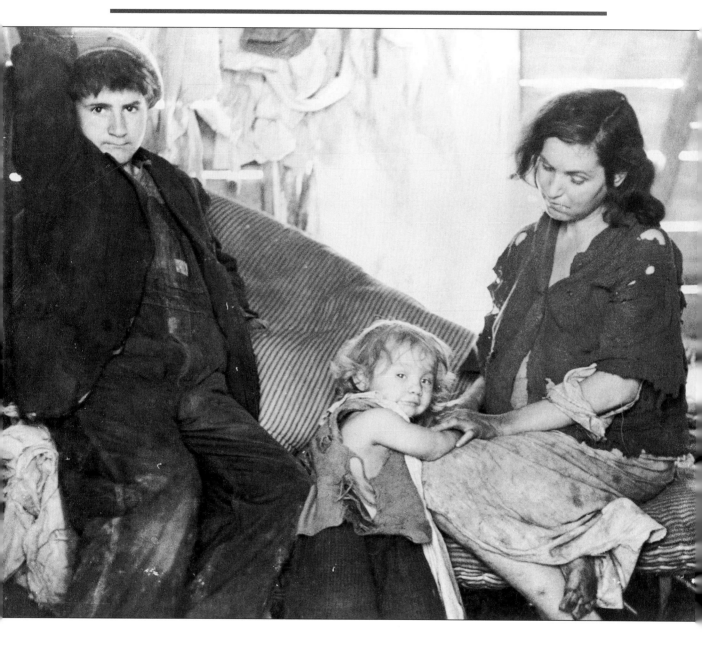

What do you feel when you see this picture? It could have been an illustration of President Roosevelt's famous description of one-third of America as "ill-housed, ill-clad, ill-nourished." (Carl Mydans)

were kept during the daytime in the car. There was no possible shelter. . . . The mother told the worker on the survey that she had been known as the best housekeeper in her home town. . . .

Many of the families camping along the irrigation ditches were using the ditchwater for drinking purposes as well as using the side of the ditch as a toilet. In February a child from one of these families was taken to the County Hospital with spinal meningitis. There had been no quarantine and the other members of the family were mixing with their neighbors. Children dressed in rags, their hands encrusted with dirt, complexions pasty white, their teeth quite rotted, were observed in these camps.

One blind baby was not able to sit up. The mother said, We've never had enough money for doctors. I don't know what's the matter with baby or why she's blind. She certainly is poorly. I don't know what the relief will do. We're transients. My husband does farming or anything. We picked cotton in Arizona for a little while after we left Oklahoma but didn't earn much. We thought if we came to California we would be able to pick peas, but when we arrived all the company camps were full and they wouldn't let us in. We have been here a month and my husband hasn't had a thing to do yet. Now the health doctor gave us notice to move no later than today. I wonder where we can go.

In the San Joaquin Valley of California, cotton was one of the principal products in the 1930s. An irrigated crop, California cotton had a yield three times as great as the national average yield per acre. It cost less per pound to grow cotton here than anywhere else in the United States. It took 35,000 workers to pick the cotton crop, with big families highly favored over single workers. The reason? Owners could pay children an even lower rate than their parents.

Carey McWilliams, the state commissioner of immigration and

Children, too, picked cotton in the San Joaquin Valley of California. Child labor meant cheaper labor.

housing, inspected conditions at the immigrant camps in the spring of 1939. He reported:

In March and April, 1939, I was in the San Joaquin Valley, inspecting labor camps. There are some 470 cotton camps in the valley. According to a formula used by the growers, each cabin in a cotton camp is theoretically supposed to account for 800 pounds of cotton a day during the picking season. Since the average worker can only pick about 200 pounds a day, it follows that each cabin must contain about four active pickers. Overcrowding is inevitable. The cabins are all one-room frame shacks and I have frequently

A family of cotton pickers in the doorway of their one-room shack.

found as many as eight and ten people living in one cabin. Some of the cotton camps are quite large; as many as 2,000 pickers will sometimes be found in a single camp. There are Negro camps, Mexican camps, and White-American camps. . . .

Most of the camps should ordinarily be vacant in March or April since the cotton picking is over by January. But in the spring of 1939 the camps were 40 percent occupied. Most of the occupants told me that they had been stranded at the end of the season and had to stay on in the camp. With scarcely an exception, they were all on relief, and in many cases the growers were getting $5 a month rent for the cabins from the State Relief Administration. Most of the large cotton camps are located miles away from the nearest major highway, and some of them, in the winter and spring, are islands in a sea of mud and water. There is a characteristic odor about a cotton camp that defies description. For days after an inspection trip of this kind, I could still imagine that the odor of the camps somehow clung to my clothes. . . .

McWilliams talked to the cotton pickers:

The story they had to tell was undeniably impressive. Working ten hours a day in the fields chopping cotton, they had to pay their own transportation expenses to and from work, sometimes commuting ten and fifteen miles each way. For the miserable shacks in which most of them lived, rents averaged $8 to $10 a month. Utility charges were high; food was high. Under these circumstances, no man could support a family on 20 cents an hour. Average earnings for the season, at this rate, would actually be less than the meager allowances they received on relief.

With migrants pouring into Madera County since 1933, by 1939 its population had nearly doubled. The growers who had come to California from Texas, Georgia, and Mississippi in the early twenties had no sympathy for these uprooted newcomers. They called them "Okies," regardless of their place of origin, and put them scornfully at the bottom of the social ladder. McWilliams found:

Migrants discovered, of course, that there was no place for them in the rural economy of the region except as farm workers. There were no homesteads to be claimed, no free lands awaiting settlement. The price of good farm land in the county was utterly beyond the reach of the average migrant family. Stranded in the community, migrants had to seek relief. Resentment between "residents" and "newcomers" rapidly developed. A great portion of the population of the county actually came from the same areas in the South and Southwest; they were all citizens, all farmers, all "White-Americans." They shared to a considerable degree the same prejudices, the same taboos, the same aspirations. Yet the residents vehemently contended that they were "the people of Madera County"; and by inference that the Okies were "aliens." This feeling was so pronounced that in the summer of 1939 a sign appeared in the foyer of a motion picture theatre in a San Joaquin Valley town, reading: "Negroes and Okies Upstairs."

Migrant children suffered most from this kind of existence. They were weakened by poverty and poor food—a steady diet of beans, rice, fried dough, and almost no milk, fruit, or vegetables. Many of them suffered from some form of malnutrition. They died of hunger, from accidents, of sickness. A state health agency surveyed a group of 831 migrant children and found so large a number of medical problems of all kinds that they called it a "pediatric nightmare." The often life-threatening illnesses included pneumonia, polio, boils, impetigo, whooping cough, heatstroke, meningitis, tuberculosis. Little could be done to cure or prevent

Children of migrant families suffered the most from that life. Extreme poverty was at the root of their troubles. It led inevitably to sickness, stunted growth, a lack of education, and a sense of rootlessness.

such illnesses, for antibiotics, and many of the vaccines, had yet to be invented.

Once, in the fall of 1936, an intestinal flu swept through the valley. Hundreds of children ran fevers, developed diarrhea, went into convulsions, and died.

Just as troubling for migrant parents was the education of their children. Or rather the lack of it. Moving about so often, so quickly, made schooling almost impossible. Hardly did a child enter a local school, than he or she was taken out because the family had to follow the crops. Some parents began to notice that their kids could not write a decent English sentence. A desolate feeling sank in: What did the future hold for their children? Not the progress from generation to generation that most Americans had come to expect, but a falling back.

What to do about migrants? Would anyone hold out a helping hand? California insisted they must wait a year before becoming eligible for relief ($16 a month). If within that time they were in serious distress, they got temporary aid, and the offer of free transportation back home. But the home states were not welcoming; they put up barriers against their return. Most of the migrants chose to scrape by until they established settlement in California and the right to public assistance.

The only government agency—state or federal—to try to supply a solution, however partial, to the migrant problem was the Farm Security Administration (FSA). (The Taylor-Lange reports helped bring this about.) The FSA in 1935 began to build sanitary, government-supervised camps. Some were set permanently in heavy work areas. Other were mobile—designed to be moved along with the crops. The permanent ones (ten of them operating by 1939) furnished solid tent bases, an isolation unit for the sick, a clinic and a nursery, an assembly hall, an incinerator, a pump house, laundry tubs, showers, and sanitary toilets. This cost the government about $400 per family. The camps were run by the migrants themselves under FSA supervision. The camp charge to the tenants was

In this close-up of a migratory worker in California, Dorothea Lange catches a facial expression that tells us much about the life he knows.

only ten cents a week or two hours of work on camp maintenance. That rental fee went for entertainment and emergencies.

Trying to get the powerful figures in California's business and politics to do more for the migrants, Paul Taylor appealed to them in a speech at the Commonwealth Club on April 15, 1938. After outlining the problems, he concluded:

Thus far I have answered your question, "What shall we do with them?" in these terms. We cannot stop them from coming by refusing to give them relief in California when they need it. They

A migrant family takes it easy in front of their clean new home given to them by the FSA. The reports of Dorothea Lange and Paul Taylor helped create the FSA camps.

are forced from their own communities; directly and indirectly we invite them; we use their labor. Not only are they here by tens of thousands of families, but more are coming.

These simple facts we must face. It follows as elementary, therefore, that whether we like them or not, we dare not tolerate in our midst their hunger and the malnutrition of their children, their unsanitary living conditions, and their disease. Neither the state of California nor the United States can postpone or avoid this responsibility.

Although some among the elite showed compassion, most did not. They did their best to prevent the migrant workers from organizing to improve their conditions. True, the notion of joining a union wasn't easy to get across in the first place. Many of the Okies were independent-minded individualists raised to take care of themselves. To them this labor in the fields was only a temporary necessity. Even so, growers like the DiGiorgios wanted no part of unions. They tried to divide the workers by ethnic groups to lessen the chance they would unite. And they succeeded to a degree. For Okies became strikebreakers in some clashes between growers and laborers. When an agricultural workers union was formed, the growers charged it was run by Communists, and many Okies swallowed the propaganda.

Though the union membership never grew large, the fact that it existed at all angered the growers. They mustered the tools of antilabor warfare—finks, goon squads, tear gas, bribes, espionage—to break up the union.

The chief instrument of the big growers was the Associated Farmers organization. An instance of how it operated can be seen in the San Joaquin Valley, where the cotton growers, united in the Associated Farmers, had fixed a very low wage rate. That year a man and wife picking cotton for sixty-six days—the length of the average season—at the going rate of eighty cents per hundred pounds, would make $140.57. But the growers flatly refused to raise the rate, even by pennies. So the migrant pickers—some eight to ten thousand of them—voted through their union to strike for a higher wage. Within a week cotton production began to drop rapidly. The growers, enraged by the threat to their profits, organized a private army to break the strike. On the morning of October 22, 1939, the migrant pickers held a strike rally in the public park in Madera.

Over six hundred men, armed with clubs, pick handles, rubber hoses, and auto cranks rushed into the park and proceeded to break up

A jobless migrant on the edge of a pea field in California's Imperial Valley. Would he join a union to better his conditions? Or would he go it alone, as he always had before?

Who Wanted Them?

Migrant workers came on the scene as an important source of seasonal labor during World War I, when farms were short of manpower. In the East and Midwest they were mainly newly arrived immigrants. Farther west, in California, they were both native-born Americans and Mexicans brought in for short periods to work for very low wages.

But farmers developed new methods for producing intensive crops like fruit and vegetables. The change was made possible by heavy investments in irrigation, farm machinery, and other equipment that only wealthy individuals or corporations could afford. To make such investments profitable you had to apply it only to large areas. That led to much bigger farms and tighter control of ownership. Giant corporations and banks ran the show. "Agribusiness," they called it.

This caused great changes in the labor picture. The small farmer with limited acreage found it very hard to compete with the huge farms. Field hands, to whom the small farmer had given steady work, were no longer needed. A new type of worker replaced the yearly hired hands. These were the seasonal workers. Their job was to harvest those crops that required hand labor rather than machines. The work they did was too delicate for machines and too hard and dirty and low-paid for any but the dispossessed—those whose choice was either to work or to starve. Their labor had to be done quickly so that the crops could be processed and marketed before they might spoil or rot.

It was this labor market that the Dust Bowlers—homeless, voteless nomads—entered. Who wanted them—except at harvesttime?

an orderly strike meeting. The county sheriff stood by, doing nothing, as scores of strikers were beaten up so badly they had to be rushed to the hospital. The sheriff made no arrests and said later he could not identify any of the assailants. Yet photos taken the day of the assault showed him in company with the mob's ringleaders. He arrested 124 strikers on purely technical charges and held them on as much as $2,500 bail each. Not a single grower was arrested, although they had paraded without a permit, committed assaults, and fomented a riot.

The law for the migrants was one thing. For the growers, it was something else.

After the riot the strike soon collapsed. The migrant pickers drifted back to work at their old low rate. The gins were soon running at full speed, and a bumper crop was harvested.

A little gas station at a crossroads in Kern County, California, 1938. The sign tells the world what the independent-minded owner thinks.

Seven

A New Deal

THE MAGNITUDE OF THE GREAT DEPRESSION DEFIES ATTEMPTS TO CONvey the human suffering of those years. So too did it defy the New Deal's attempts to deal with it. The administration of Franklin Delano Roosevelt devised many measures to ease the pain, to end the unemployment, to help the farmers, but the pace of action and the scope of programs never matched the needs.

What the government offered was an alphabet soup of acronyms—FERA, AAA, TVA, CWA, CCC, PWA, REA, FSA, WPA—that provided some relief. But the government never dealt with the fundamental issues: overproduction and underconsumption. These two related facts were at the root of economic disorder. And no one in power wished to tamper with them.

"Business was business," of course. The Depression was no one person's fault. But people felt it was time that government—if it was truly representative of all the people—should step in. So in November of 1932, three years after the onset of the Depression, the people chose Roosevelt over Herbert Hoover because he promised change. FDR carried all but six states, getting 22 million votes against Hoover's 15 million.

That large majority believed both business and government needed to develop a social conscience. And both should be made to work for the benefit of all. They knew the goal of business was profits and that government, up to that time, had never wished to interfere with that goal, no matter what the cost. But this crisis was too deep, too terrible, too enduring to leave things as they were. Now Roosevelt promised a "New Deal." And the national mood favored anyone who promised to act, to move, to do something, anything.

When FDR took the oath of office, he told the nation, "The only thing we have to fear is fear itself." He acted, and swiftly. Congress gave him broad executive powers to wage war against the emergency. In one hundred days the legislators passed bill after bill, many of them half-thought-out or experimental, but all aimed at bringing about economic recovery.

Federal relief came first, and then billions of dollars to provide public works so that some of the unemployed could find jobs again. There were about 13 million people unemployed in 1933, or one-fourth of the labor force. But in 1938 over nine million were still unemployed. Productive capacity still outpaced consumer ability to buy. Nothing was done to revise the income and tax structure, which as always favored the rich. It was only by vastly increased consumption that industrial productivity could be reconciled with full employment.

As late as 1939 only one-tenth of personal income was subject to income tax. This at a time when the wealthiest 20 percent held nearly 50 percent of all income.

The New Deal's response to the misery of the Depression was always hesitant and hit-or-miss because of mistaken optimism that economic

At an outdoor rally in Georgia, 1933, President Roosevelt is greeted warmly by people overjoyed by the New Deal's program to lift the country out of the Depression.

recovery would come inevitably, and soon. As it faced the costs of experimental programs, always greater than expected, the New Deal created one agency after another. There were some real results: people were put to work. Roads, parks, airports, hospitals, school buildings, courthouses, libraries, bridges, and other public structures were built. But no major dent was made in the jobless figure.

The New Deal policy on agriculture is one example of the government's inability to solve a critical problem. As we've seen, by 1940 a million people had fled the Dust Bowl regions to migrate toward the Pacific

coast. Government provided a modest work-camp program, but most of the Dust Bowlers labored on the great corporate farms under conditions approaching peonage.

Southern tenant farmers and sharecroppers benefited little if at all from the policy of the Agricultural Adjustment Administration (AAA). Intending to raise the price of farm products by cutting back production, the AAA paid money to landowners. Since most of the actual farming was done by croppers or tenants, who did not own the land they worked on, the AAA benefits did not reach them. Just the reverse: the government

New Deal programs gave the unemployed useful, decently paid work. Far left: WPA (Works Progress Administration) workers rebuild one of New York City's avenues. Center: Young men of the Civilian Conservation Corps clear burned-out areas of forest in the state of Washington. Bottom: An artist employed by the Federal Arts Project creates a mural for the California State Building in Los Angeles.

program paid a premium to remove land from production, making it profitable for landlords to drive croppers and tenants off the land and into even deeper poverty and despair. As for the large farmers, they cultivated their fewer acres more intensely, with the result that the total crop was not reduced very much.

In April 1935 the Resettlement Administration (RA) was set up to tackle the problem of rural poverty. Its aim was to remove croppers and tenants from submarginal land and resettle them on good soil with government-supplied equipment and seed to give them a fresh start. The RA meant to move half a million families, but it only managed to move about 4,500. Why? Because Congress never gave it enough money.

Two years later another new agency, the Farm Security Administration (FSA), was launched. It loaned money to tenants and sharecroppers so that they could buy their own farms. And it helped the Dust Bowlers by establishing the work camps we've described. By 1941 the FSA had put nearly $1 billion into its various programs, but it never had enough money to do more than scratch the surface of rural poverty.

Why? Because southern landowners, along with large northern food processors and textile manufacturers, did not want to see any basic change in the social structure. Votes count when political decisions are made. But most of the poor farmers seldom voted, while the landowners and food processors had many good friends in the halls of Congress. The agencies set up to help reduce poverty and suffering never got more than a fraction of the sums needed.

While there was little to be done about the tragedy of the Dust Bowl, something could be done to prevent such a disaster from happening again. Through the Civilian Conservation Corps (CCC) 2.5 million young, unemployed men from eighteen to twenty-five and eight thousand women were transplanted to western prairies and forests. They built many of the smaller dams that held back streams and river branches, controlling the floods that had carried off crumbling topsoil. They also planted a huge

A federal agency designed to bolster the weak agricultural industry paid out crop benefits to be shared between planters and their sharecroppers. But some landowners evicted these farmworkers to avoid paying them benefits. Hundreds of homeless families huddled together in improvised camps between Missouri and Arkansas.

About 250,000 men were taken off the unemployment rolls for a New Deal program of reforestation. Here workers pull up two-year-old fir trees to ship them to various parts of the country for transplanting.

shelterbelt of trees that stretched from Canada to Texas. Many minor shelterbelts were planted across states and counties too. The trees helped break the winds, hold water in the soil, and keep the soil itself in place. This was one of the most successful of all the New Deal programs.

It was too late to help the Dust Bowlers of the early thirties, but the complex program of dams, lakes, and national forests provided strong protection against any black blizzard in the future. Part of that soil conservation program was the education of farmers in how to avoid soil erosion in the future. Farmers were taught about crop rotation, strip farming, and how to give the land a rest. They learned to view the land as a national treasure, which no one has the right to ruin for future generations. It's never easy to ensure that such ideals will be realized. There are constant conflicts between those who want to preserve and protect the national domain and those whose hunger for profits at whatever price lead them to litter, to pollute, to poison the land and what it nurtures. But the New Deal did create the climate and some of the methods through which conservation programs of the future might succeed.

As the 1930s began, the United States was the only major industrial country without a program to provide health insurance, old age pensions, and unemployment insurance. Under the pressure of prolonged hard times, Congress in 1935 finally passed the Social Security Act. It provided old age and survivor insurance to be paid for by a small tax on both employer and employee, a cooperative federal-state system of unemployment compensation, and federal grants to the states to assist in caring for the disabled and supporting dependent children.

The Social Security Act was a beginning, at long last, but it excluded many who needed help most, such as farm laborers and domestic workers, and it failed to offer insurance covering sickness. Yet it was a landmark in American social legislation, for it meant government was accepting some responsibility for the care of its citizens.

One major advance made during the thirties was the new deal government offered labor. In 1935 Congress adopted the National Labor Relations Act (NLRA). It outlawed blacklisting and a number of other antilabor practices and asserted labor's right to organize and bargain collectively. The act didn't require workers to join unions, but it made the federal government a regulator in management-labor relations. The result

Eleanor Roosevelt functioned as her husband's eyes and ears because FDR, handicapped by polio, could not easily get around the country to check on the progress of the many federal projects. After seeing the terrible living conditions of the migrants in the squatter camps, here she inspects an FSA camp to make a comparison.

was a swift rise in the size and strength of the trade union movement.

Important too for working people was the passage of the Fair Labor Standards Act (FLSA) of 1938. It set a minimum wage for all industries engaged in interstate commerce and a maximum number of hours for the work week. Here too, however, farm laborers and domestic servants were excluded. The law also banned child labor in enterprises engaged in interstate commerce.

In the thirties the African-American unemployment rate was three times greater than that of whites. And blacks often received lower welfare payments than whites. Segregation continued in every field, including government-sponsored facilities. Two major civil rights bills of the era—one outlawing lynching and the other abolishing the poll tax—were not adopted by Congress. President Roosevelt did not push them, partly because he was dependent on the support of the solid South and feared he would antagonize southern congressmen whose backing he needed for other New Deal measures.

Franklin D. Roosevelt's First Inaugural, March 4, 1933

This is pre-eminently the time to speak the truth, the whole truth, frankly and boldly. Nor need we shrink from honestly facing conditions in our country today. This great nation will endure as it has endured, will revive and will prosper.

So first of all let me assert my firm belief that the only thing we have to fear is fear itself—nameless, unreasoning, unjustified terror which paralyzes needed efforts to convert retreat into advance.

In every dark hour of our national life a leadership of frankness and vigor has met with that understanding and support of the people themselves which is essential to victory. I am convinced that you will again give that support to leadership in these critical days.

In such a spirit on my part and on yours we face our common difficulties. They concern, thank God, only material things. Values have shrunken to fantastic levels; taxes have risen; our ability to pay has fallen, government of all kinds is faced by serious curtailment of income; the means of exchange are frozen in the currents of trade; the withered leaves of industrial enterprise lie on every side; farmers find no markets for their products; the savings of many years in thousands of families are gone.

More important, a host of unemployed citizens face the grim problem of existence, and an equally great number toil with little return. Only a foolish optimist can deny the dark realities of the moment.

Yet our distress comes from no failure of substance. We are stricken by no plague of locusts. Compared with the perils which our forefathers conquered because they believed and were not afraid, we have still much to be thankful for. Nature still offers her bounty and human efforts have multiplied it. Plenty is at our doorstep, but a generous use of it languishes in the very sight of the supply.

Primarily, this is because the rulers of the exchange of mankind's goods have failed through their own stubbornness and their own incompetence, have admitted their failure and abdicated. . . .

They have no vision, and when there is no vision the people perish. . . .

The joy and moral stimulation of work no longer must be forgotten in the mad chase of evanescent profits. . . .

This nation asks for action, and action now.

Our greatest primary task is to put people to work. This is no unsolvable problem if we face it wisely and courageously. . . .

The task can be helped by definite efforts to raise the values of agricultural products and with this the power to purchase the output of our cities.

It can be helped by preventing realistically the tragedy of the growing loss, through foreclosure, of our small homes and our farms.

It can be helped by the insistence that the Federal, State and local governments act forthwith on the demand that their cost be drastically reduced.

It can be helped by the unifying of relief activities which today are often scattered, uneconomical and unequal. It can be helped by national planning for and supervision of all forms of transportation and of communications and other utilities which have a definitely public character.

There are many ways in which it can be helped, but it can never be helped merely by talking about it. We must act, and act quickly.

Finally, in our progress toward a resumption of work we require two safeguards against a return of the evils of the old order; there must be a strict supervision of all banking and credits and investments; there must be an end to speculation with other people's money, and there must be provision for an adequate but sound currency. . . .

The basic thought that guides these specific means of national recovery is not narrowly nationalistic.

It is the insistence, as a first consideration, upon the interdependence of the various elements in, and parts of, the United States—a recognition of the old and permanently important manifestation of the American spirit of the pioneer.

It is the way to recovery. It is the immediate way. It is the strongest assurance that the recovery will endure.

The president and Mrs. Roosevelt on their way back to the White House after his third inauguration in 1941

Shipyard workers coming off their shift in Richmond, California, in 1942. With the outbreak of World War II and the intense demand for more labor in war production, many men and women, only recently migrants, were now acquiring new skills and held secure, well-paying jobs. (Dorothea Lange)

Eight

From Picking Fruit to Making Weapons

ON SEPTEMBER 1, 1939, GERMANY'S ARMED FORCES INVADED POLAND. The Second World War had begun. Students of foreign affairs had expected that the rise of totalitarian powers in Europe—Fascism in Italy and Nazism in Germany—preaching the necessity of war to expand territory and power, would inevitably lead to armed conflict that could draw in the whole world. But with the memory of the devastating loss of millions of lives in World War I still fresh (it had ended only twenty-one years before), a majority of Americans wished to have no international entanglements. Congress in 1937 adopted the Neutrality Act, a move to isolate the United States from other people's quarrels. But President Roosevelt, expecting the worst, pushed through Congress a hike in the defense budget and approval for the sales of arms to France and Britain, allies against Nazi leader Adolf Hitler.

Even before the Japanese attacked Pearl Harbor on December 7,

1941, hurling America into the war, preparations to arm the nation's European allies for war had begun to ease the burden of the Great Depression. Production of munitions gave the American economy its first sure revival. The United States soon developed into the arsenal of democracy for all its allies. Industrial production zoomed by almost 100 percent.

When Hitler's tanks rolled into Poland in 1939, there were still about nine million unemployed in America. The New Deal, with all its agencies and experiments, had failed to reach the goal of full employment. It was not until 1943—two years after Pearl Harbor—that everyone who wanted a job was able to find one.

Military spending got us out of the Depression. And it would be a major factor in keeping us out of depression for decades to come.

The unemployed or partially employed, including the Dust Bowlers, found jobs in shipbuilding or aircraft plants. So badly was labor power needed (with millions drafted into military service), that two-income families became quite common.

The Dust Bowlers became permanent Californians. They had come to California on the same wave of hope that inspires everyone to migrate—to find a better life. "Displaced, dispossessed, despised, they had nevertheless prevailed," wrote the California historian Kevin Starr. "Already, by 1940, in little Oklahomas throughout the southern San Joaquin, a new people, a new type of Californian, had its version of the California dream.

"During the next five years, the war years, twice as many Oklahomans came to California as arrived between 1935 and 1940, but no one took special notice, for willing workers were needed desperately in the shipyards and the airplane and munitions factories of the wartime state."

The factories in the fields still needed migrant labor to pick their fruits and vegetables at harvesttime. With the Okies now employed full time at decent wages in war production plants, the growers turned to another source of labor power desperate to work under any conditions.

A Dust Bowl farmer who migrated to California years before faces a new and better life of full-time employment, as the shipyards and aircraft plants make real the dream of prosperity. (Dorothea Lange)

These were Mexicans or Mexican Americans. Before the war they had been but a small percentage of the migrant workers. Now they changed the complexion of the people in the fields from white to brown.

As for the Okies, assimilated into Californian life, they had become just another part of the state's richly diverse mosaic.

Bibliography

Aaron, Daniel and Robert Bendiner. *The Strenuous Decade*. New York: Anchor, 1970.

Adamic, Louis. *My America*. New York: Da Capo, 1976.

Allen, Frederick Lewis. *Since Yesterday*. New York: HarperCollins, 1986.

Baldwin, Sidney. *Poverty and Politics: The Rise and Decline of the FSA*. Chapel Hill, NC: University of North Carolina Press, 1968.

Boyer, Richard O. and Herbert Morais. *Labor's Untold Story*. New York: Cameron, 1958.

Coles, Robert. *Doing Documentary Work*. New York: Oxford, 1997.

Dickenson, James R. *Home on the Range: A Century on the High Plains*. Lawrence, KS: University of Kansas Press, 1996.

Ellis, Edward Robb. *A Nation in Torment: The Great American Depression, 1929–1939*. New York: Kodansha, 1995.

Garraty, John A. *Unemployment in History*. New York: Harper, 1978.

Ganzel, Bill. *Dust Bowl Descent*. Lincoln, NE: University of Nebraska Press, 1984.

Goldston, Robert. *The Great Depression: The U.S. in the Thirties*. Indianapolis, IN: Bobbs Merrill, 1968.

Hallgren, Mauritz. *Seeds of Revolt*. New York: Knopf, 1933.

Heaps, Willard A. *Wandering Workers*. New York: Crown, 1968.

Hurt, R. Douglas. *The Dust Bowl: An Agricultural and Social History*. Chicago: Nelson-Hall, 1981.

Josephson, Matthew. *Infidel in the Temple*. New York: Knopf, 1967.

Komisar, Lucy. *Down and Out in the USA: A History of Public Welfare*. New York: Watts, 1977.

Lange, Dorothea and Paul S. Taylor. *An American Exodus: A Record of Human Erosion in the Thirties*. New Haven, CT: Yale University Press, 1969.

Leuchtenberg, William E., ed. *The New Deal: A Documentary History*. New York: Harper, 1968.

Levin, Howard M. and Katherine Northrup, eds. *Dorothea Lange: FSA Photographs, 1935–39*. 2 vols. Glencoe, IL: Textfiche Press, 1980.

Lisca, Peter, ed. *The Grapes of Wrath: Text and Criticism*. New York: Penguin, 1997.

McElvaine, Robert S. *The Great Depression: America, 1929–1941*. New York: Times Books, 1994.

McWilliams, Carey. *The Education of Carey McWilliams*. New York: Simon & Schuster, 1978.

————. *Factories in the Field*. Boston: Little, Brown, 1939.

MacLeish, Archibald. *Land of the Free*. New York: Da Capo, 1977.

Meltzer, Milton. *Dorothea Lange: A Photographer's Life*. Syracuse, NY: Syracuse University Press, 1999.

Mitchell, Broadus. *Depression Decade: 1929–1941*. Armonk, NY: Sharpe, 1989.

Morgan, Dan. *Rising in the West*. New York: Knopf, 1992.

Rorty, James. *Where Life is Better: An Unsentimental American Journey*. New York: John Day, 1936.

Shannon, David A. *The Great Depression*. Magnolia, MA: Peter Smith, 1980.

Starr, Kevin. *Endangered Dreams: The Great Depression in California*. New York: Oxford University Press, 1996.

Steichen, Edward, ed. *The Bitter Years: 1935–1941. Rural American as Seen by the Photographers of the FSA*. New York: Museum of Modern Art, 1962.

Stott, William. *Documentary Expression and Thirties America*. Chicago: University of Chicago Press, 1986.

Wecter, Dixon. *The Age of the Great Depression: 1929–1941*. New York: AMS Press, 1999.

Worster, Donald. *Dust Bowl: The Southern Plains in the 1930s*. New York: Oxford University Press, 1982.

Further Reading

Those who wish to learn more about the Dust Bowlers and the decade of the Great Depression they were part of may find the following books helpful. Fiction too can often bring us closer to the inmost feelings of the people who lived through those years. *The Grapes of Wrath*, by John Steinbeck (New York: Viking, 1939), opened the eyes of untold thousands to grim reality, through telling the story of the Joad family, Dust Bowl refugees. The novel has become a classic and earned the author the Nobel Prize in literature.

Andryszewski, Tricia. *The Dust Bowl: Disaster on the Plains*. Brookfield, CT: The Millbrook Press, 1994.

Davies, Nancy M. *The Stock Market Crash of Nineteen Twenty-nine*. Parsippany, NJ: New Discovery, 1994.

Glassman, Bruce. *The Crash of Twenty-nine and the New Deal*. Morristown, NJ: Silver Burdett, 1985.

Meltzer, Milton. *Brother, Can You Spare a Dime?: The Great Depression 1929–1933*. New York: Facts on File, 1991.

Migneco, Ronald and Timothy L. Biel. *The Crash of 1929*. San Diego: Lucent, 1989.

Stanley, Jerry. *Children of the Dust Bowl: The True Story of the School at Weedpatch Camp*. New York: Crown Books for Young Readers, 1992.

Stewart, Gail B. *The New Deal*. Parsippany, NJ: New Discovery, 1993.

Wormser, Richard L. *Growing Up in the Great Depression*. New York: Atheneum, 1995.

Index